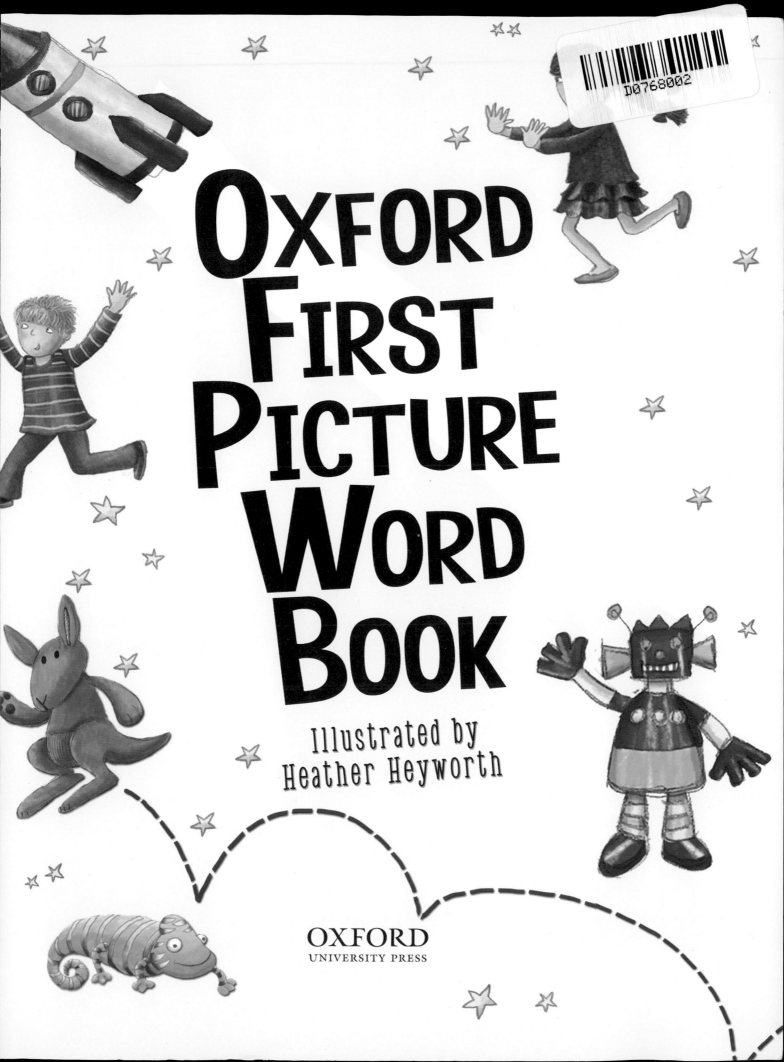

OXFORD FIRST PICTURE WORD BOOK

Illustrated by
Heather Heyworth

OXFORD
UNIVERSITY PRESS

OXFORD
UNIVERSITY PRESS

Great Clarendon Street, Oxford OX2 6DP

Oxford University Press is a department of the University of Oxford.
It furthers the University's objective of excellence in research,
scholarship, and education by publishing worldwide in

Oxford   New York

Auckland   Cape Town   Dar es Salaam   Hong Kong   Karachi
Kuala Lumpur   Madrid   Melbourne   Mexico City   Nairobi
New Delhi   Shanghai   Taipei   Toronto

With offices in

Argentina   Austria   Brazil   Chile   Czech Republic   France   Greece
Guatemala   Hungary   Italy   Japan   Poland   Portugal   Singapore
South Korea   Switzerland   Thailand   Turkey   Ukraine   Vietnam

Oxford is a registered trade mark of Oxford University Press
in the UK and in certain other countries

Illustrations © Heather Heyworth 2011
The Publisher would like to thank Lesley Pettitt for her help with text compilation.

© Oxford University Press 2011

Database right Oxford University Press (maker)

First published 2011

British Library Cataloguing in Publication Data

Data available

ISBN: 978-0-19-911716-1

1 3 5 7 9 10 8 6 4 2

Printed in China

Welcome to this first word book. Turn the pages to find first words in familiar settings. You can spot all the words illustrated in the pictures, search for the cheeky chameleon hiding in every scene, and answer the robot's questions. You can enjoy this book in a number of ways—create stories, look at the detail, and begin to recognise words for everyday favourite things.

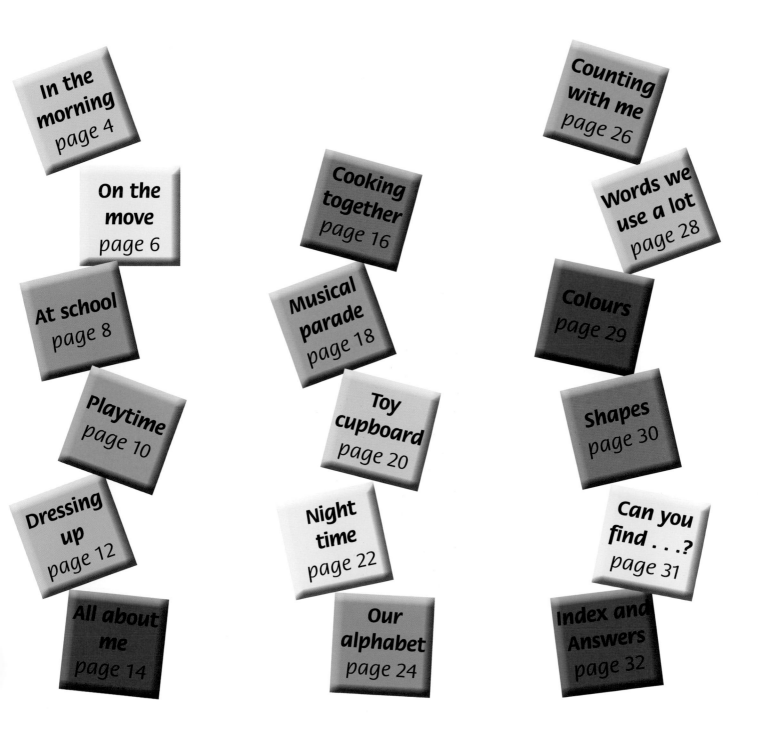

In the morning

vest

dress

T-shirt

hat

shirt

coat

jumper

scarf

shorts

umbrella

trousers

gloves

skirt

shoes

4

On the move

rocket

helicopter

boat

submarine

motorbike

bus

Can you spot and name all the things that can fly?

bicycle

tractor

recycle truck

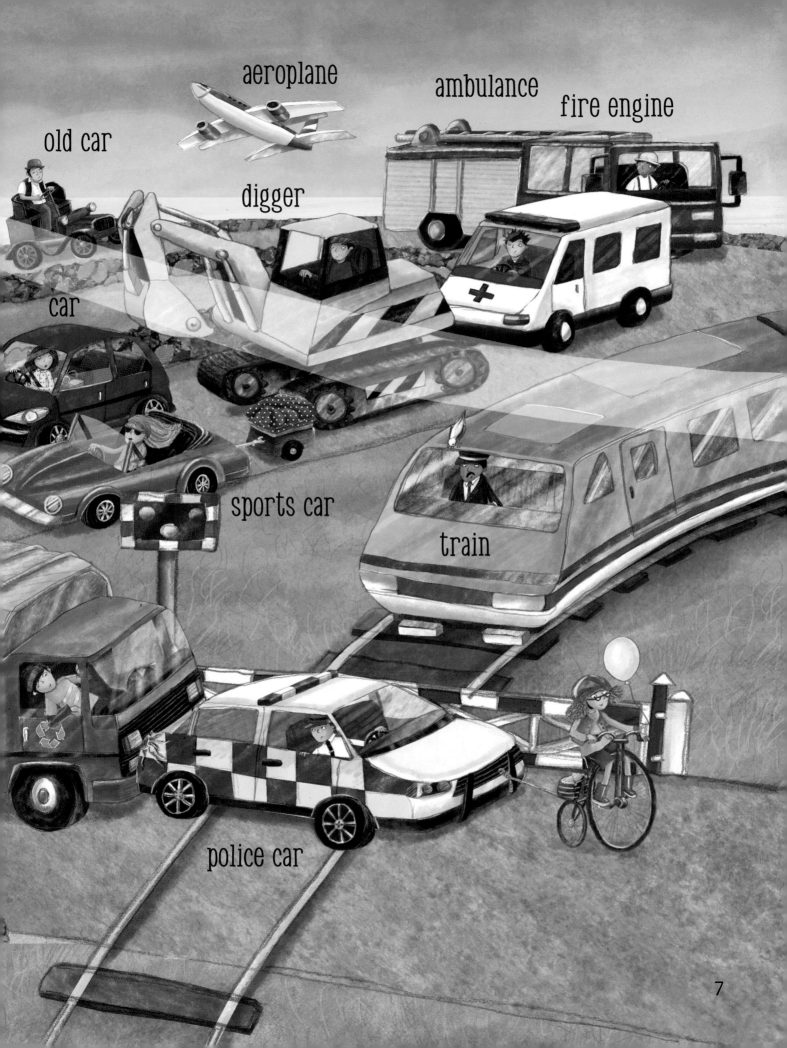

aeroplane

ambulance

fire engine

old car

digger

car

sports car

train

police car

jump

ball

kick

hop

table

chair

glue

scissors

ruler

pencils

paintbrush

paint

9

Playtime

Dressing up

Can you match all the different words to the children?

footballer   doctor   princess   ballet dancer

firefighter   astronaut   ghost   prince

police officer   racing driver   vet   cook   pirate

knight   fairy   cowgirl   builder   clown

All about me

nose   chin   eye
face   cheek   ear   tongue

14

neck   shoulder   hand   chest   leg   foot
arm   elbow   finger   tummy   knee   toe

Cooking together

butter

knife

eggs

cheese

bread

bowl

wooden spoon

flour

pastry

17

Musical parade

triangle

harp

tin whistle

trumpet

recorder

maraca

banjo

What instrument is the boy in the red shorts playing?

18

horn

accordion

cymbals

drum

bells

castanets

bass drum

band leader

19

Toy cupboard

elephant

crocodile

giraffe

fish

parrot

kangaroo

monkey

koala

mouse

penguin

tiger

zebra

panda

rhinoceros

snake

horse

hedgehog

octopus

chicken   spider   bear

21

Night time

 moon

 star

 spaceship

 planet

 curtains

 wardrobe

 clock

 telescope

 towel

 bath

 pyjamas

 toothbrush

 bed

22

Our alphabet

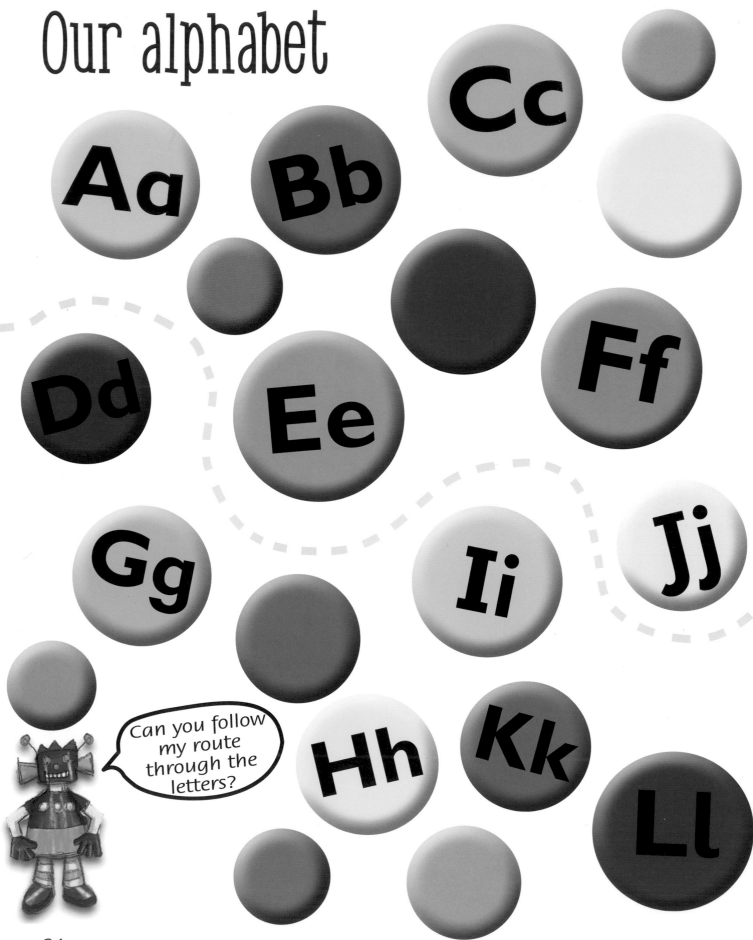

Can you follow my route through the letters?

24

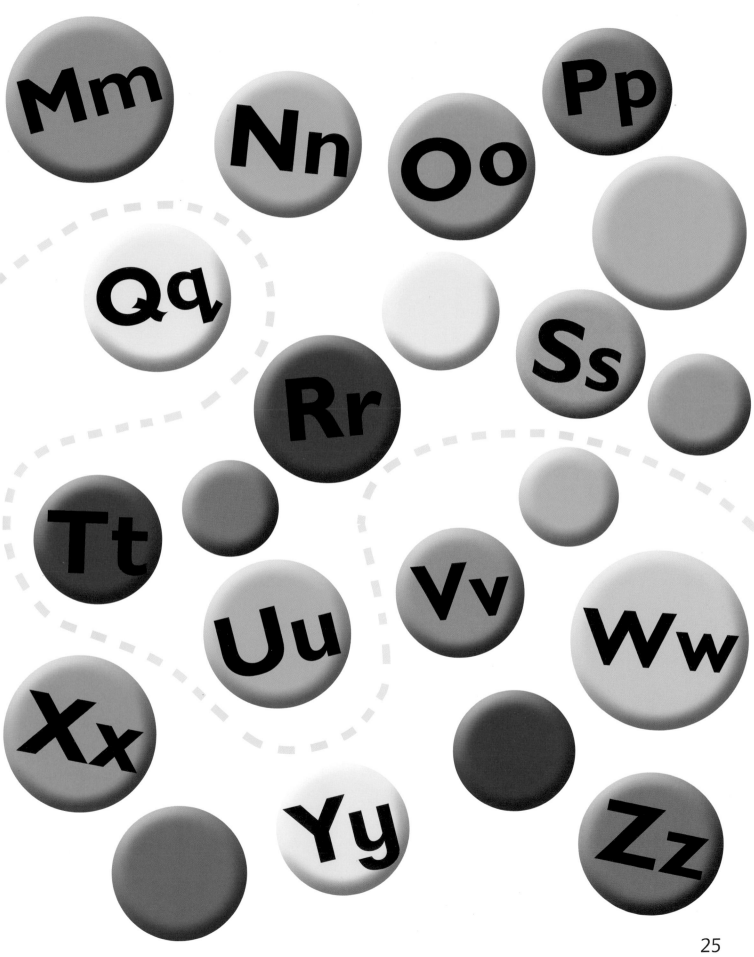

Counting with me

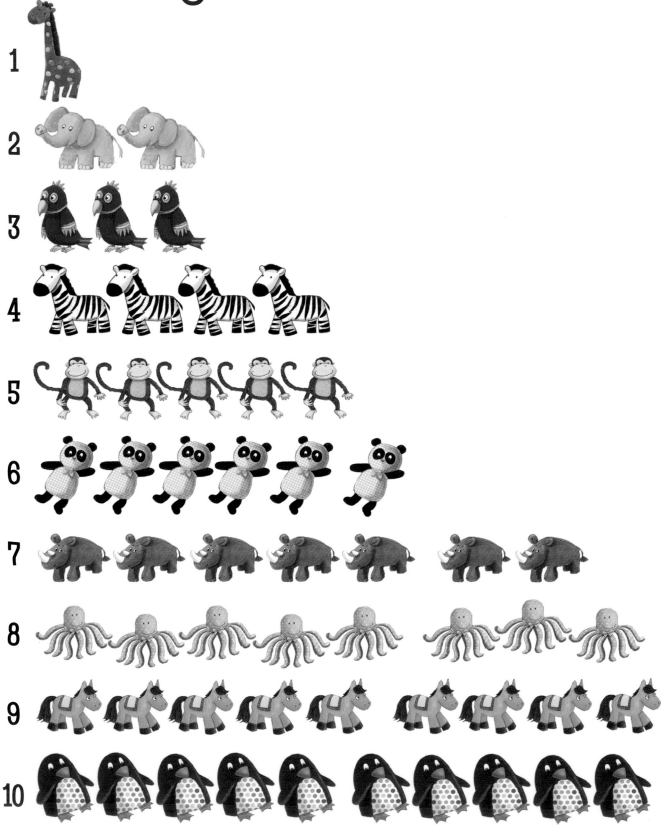

1

2

3

4

5

6

7

8

9

10

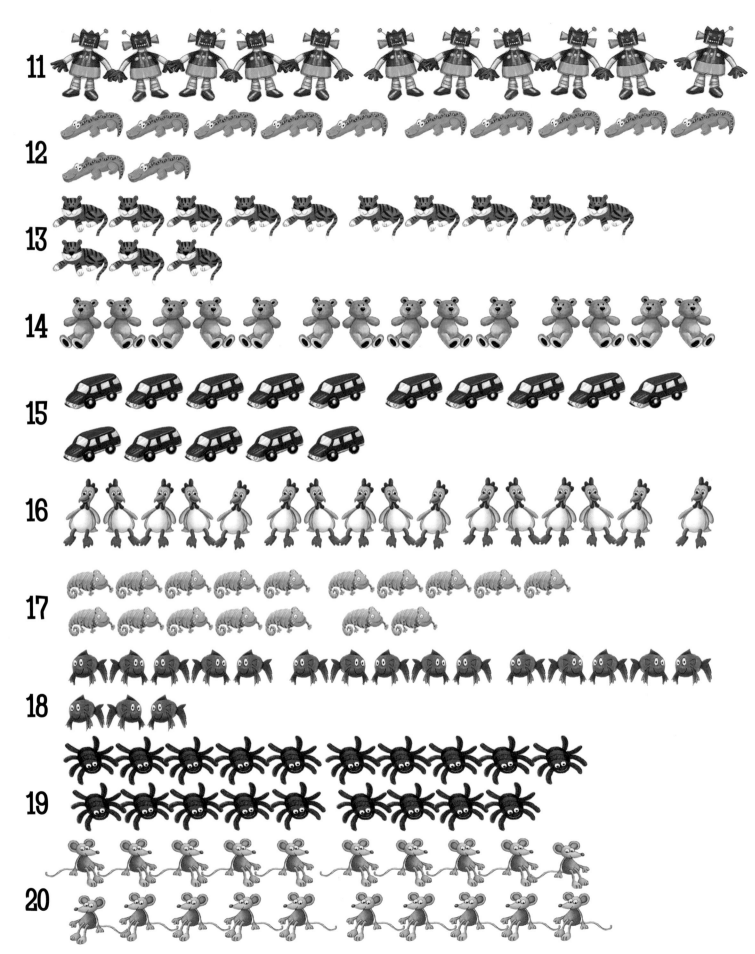

11

12

13

14

15

16

17

18

19

20

Words we use a lot

a	I	is	it	in	no
yes	to	go	of	we	me
am	you	my	he	she	they
at	up	for	the	and	are
said	went	get	all	like	see
on	can	day	play	this	was

How many words start with the letter 'a'?

Colours

green

blue

pink

brown

black and white

red

orange

purple

yellow

grey

Shapes

square

rectangle

circle

triangle

hexagon

diamond

oval

pentagon

cube

cuboid

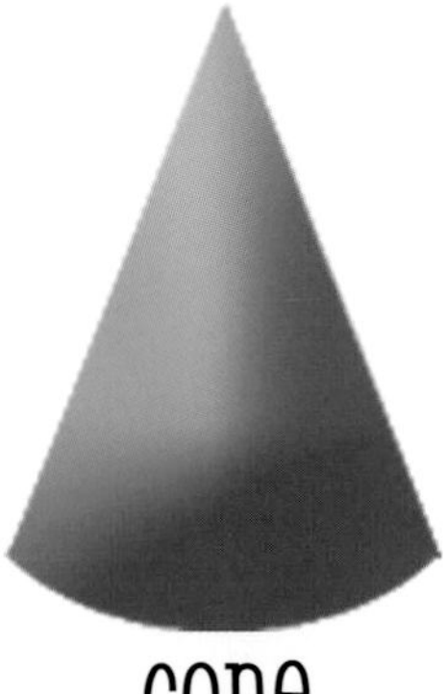

cone

pyramid

cylinder

sphere

Can you find . . . ?

Find three things that are made of plastic.

What colour is the cone on the Shapes page?

Is your favourite animal in the toy cupboard?

Can you find the cheeky chameleon lurking in every big picture?

What transport can take you on holiday?

Did you spot the animal with two horns?

The cheeky chameleon has a prickly friend who appears twice. Can you find him?

Find three things that are made of cloth.

Find three things that are made of wood.

Can you see what colour the astronaut's gloves are?

How many eggs are on the table?

Index

Answers: • Can you find the cheeky chameleon lurking in every picture? 'In the morning' - in the bath; ' On the move' - in the first bicycle's basket; 'At school' - behind the computer; 'Playtime' - in the tree; 'Dressing up' - in the clown's hair; 'All about me' - in the tyres; 'Cooking together' - on the back of the chair; 'Musical parade' - behind the harp; 'Toy cupboard' - on the top shelf; 'Night time' - in the spaceship. • What colour is the cone on the Shapes page? Blue. • How many eggs are on the table? Four. • Can you see what colour the astronaut's gloves are? Red. • A prickly animal appears twice. Can you find him? The hedgehog is in the bathroom 'In the morning', and on top of the toy cupboard. • Did you spot the animal with two horns? The rhinoceros appears in three pictures: 'In the morning', 'Toy cupboard', and 'Night time'. • What transport can take you on holiday? Aeroplane, car, bus, bicycle, motorbike, boat, sports car, train.

32